50 words about

Dinosaurs

David and Patricia Armentrout

Rourke
Publishing LLC
Vero Beach, Florida 32964

www.rourkepublishing.com

PHOTO CREDITS: © James P. Rowan Cover, pages 4, 5, 6, 7 top, 9 top, 11 top, 14, 16 top, 17 bottom, 19 bottom, 20, 22, 23, 24 top, 25 top; © Painet, Inc. pages 8 top, 10 top, 12, 15 top, 17 top, 18 top, 19 top, 21 top, 25 bottom, 26 bottom, 27 bottom, 28 top; © PhotoDisc pages 8 bottom, 13 bottom, 15 bottom, 16 bottom, 21 bottom, 28 bottom; © Armentrout pages 7 bottom, 9 bottom, 10 bottom, 11 bottom, 13 top, 18 bottom, 24 bottom, 26 top, 27 top

Editor: Frank Sloan

Cover and page design by Nicola Stratford

Library of Congress Cataloging-in-Publication Data

Armentrout, David, 1962-
  Dinosaurs / David and Patricia Armentrout.
      p. cm. — (50 words about)
Summary: Provides simple definitions for fifty words related to dinosaurs along with sample sentences using each word.
Includes bibliographical references and index.
  ISBN 1-58952-342-3
  1. Dinosaurs—Juvenile literature. [1. Dinosaurs--Dictionaries.] I. Armentrout, Patricia, 1960- II. Title.
  QE861.5 .A76 2002
  567.9--dc21
                                                                    2002002377

Printed in the USA

CG/CG

dinosaur (DY neh sor)

One of a group of extinct reptiles that lived millions of years ago.

armor

Built-in protection on an animal's body.

Some dinosaurs had heavy armor to protect their bodies.

beak

A hard, pointed outer part of the mouth.

A dinosaur's sharp beak was used to tear leaves from plants.

biped

Any animal that travels on two legs.

A biped dinosaur used its tail for balance.

bone

One of the hard, white parts of a skeleton.

Dinosaur bone fossils have been found all over the world.

breed

To produce young.

Like most animals, dinosaurs had to breed, or mate, to continue their species.

camouflage

A color or cover that makes an animal look like its surroundings.

Some dinosaurs used camouflage to hide from predators.

carnivore

An animal that eats only meat.

A carnivore used sharp teeth to tear, or rip, its food.

carnosaur

One of the huge, powerful, meat-eating dinosaurs.

A carnosaur must have been a frightening sight for smaller animals.

club

The round, bony piece of armor at the end of the tail of some dinosaurs.

Some plant-eaters used their clubs in self-defense.

cold-blooded

Animals with body temperatures that stay about the same as their surroundings.

Some dinosaurs were cold-blooded, like the modern-day alligator.

crest

A bony structure on the head of some dinosaurs.

A dinosaur's crest may have been used to attract a mate.

Cretaceous

A period of time from about 144 to 65 million years ago.

Dinosaurs and many other kinds of animals died out during the Cretaceous Period.

dig site

A place where scientists look for fossils and other remains from the past.

Scientists at the dig site carefully sift through dirt searching for dinosaur fossils.

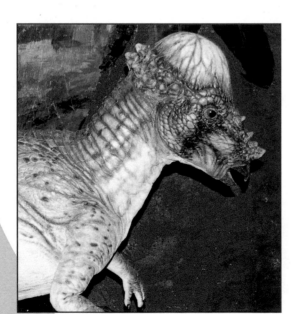

dome head

A rounded, bony skull.

The dome head on some dinosaurs was 10 inches (25.4 centimeters) thick.

egg

A shell that protects baby animals before they hatch.

A museum display shows dinosaur eggs and young.

excavate

To remove dirt and rock by digging.

These children excavate pretend dinosaur bones at a museum.

extinct

When an animal no longer lives or has died out.

Making a model of an extinct dinosaur can be a challenge.

fossil

The rock-like remains of a plant or animal that lived long ago.

A dinosaur fossil is millions of years old.

frill

A protective fold of bony skin around a dinosaur's neck.

The frill on a dinosaur may have been used to frighten predators.

habitat

The place where an animal lives.

A dinosaur's habitat depended on the creature's need for food and water.

herbivore

An animal that eats only plants.

This herbivore had small, flat teeth in the rear of its mouth for chewing.

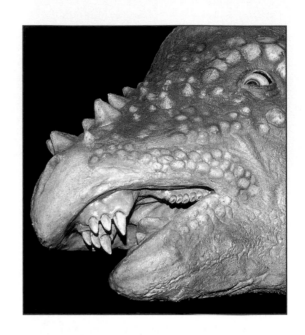

horn

A hard, bony growth on the heads of some animals.

The Triceratops had three sharp horns on its head.

hunt

To search for food.

Large dinosaurs had no choice but to hunt for food.

Ice Age

A period of time when a large part of the Earth was covered in ice.

An Ice Age may have caused some animal species to die out.

Jurassic

A period of time from about 205 to 144 million years ago.

Dinosaurs ruled the Earth during the Jurassic Period.

meteorite

A rock from space that hits Earth.

Huge meteorites sometimes hit the Earth and may have caused dinosaur extinction.

museum

A place where art, science, and historical objects are displayed.

Children learn all about dinosaurs at a museum.

omnivore

An animal that eats both plants and meat.

An omnivore dinosaur ate anything to survive.

paleontology

The scientific study of life through fossils.

To study paleontology, some scientists spend weeks at a dig site.

plates

Large, hard pieces of armor on a dinosaur's body.

The Stegosaurus is known for the row of sharp, hard plates along its back.

predator

An animal that hunts other animals for food.

Tyrannosaurus Rex was a powerful predator.

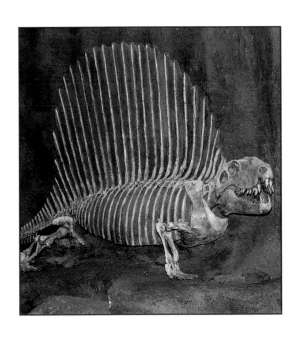

prehistoric

A time before written records were kept.

The Dimetrodon was not a dinosaur, but lived in prehistoric times.

prey

An animal that is hunted by other animals for food.

A marine reptile attacks its prey.

pterosaur

A flying reptile from the time of dinosaurs.

A pterosaur ate small dinosaurs, fish, and mammals.

remains

Parts of something that once lived.

People sometimes find dinosaur remains, such as this egg fossil.

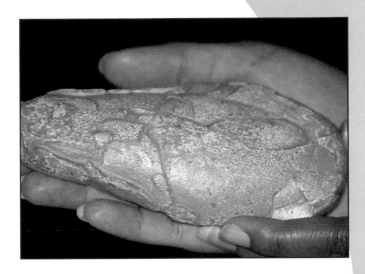

reptile

A cold-blooded animal with a backbone and scaly skin, which can be found on land or in water.

Reptiles, such as tortoises, lived during the time of dinosaurs.

sauropod

A large, long-necked plant-eating dinosaur.

Sauropods are among the largest animals ever to walk the Earth.

scales

Small, hard plates that cover the body of a fish or reptile.

Scales protected a dinosaur from small bites and cuts.

sense

A power an animal uses to learn about its surroundings.

The sense of smell and sight were important to dinosaurs.

skeleton

The framework of bones in an animal's body.

Scientists rebuild dinosaur skeletons to see what they really looked like.

skin

The tough outside layer of an animal's body.

Large dinosaurs had tough, thick skin.

skull

The bony frame of the head that protects the brain.

A Tyrannosaurus Rex skull had powerful jaws loaded with sharp teeth.

species

One certain kind of animal.

The Anantosaurus was one species of duck-billed dinosaur.

tail

A part that sticks out of the back of a dinosaur's body.

A dinosaur's tail could be used for balance and self-defense.

talons

Long, sharp claws.

Some dinosaurs had talons that they used to kill their prey.

teeth

Bony parts of the mouth used for biting and chewing.

Some dinosaur teeth were 6 inches (15.24 centimeters) long!

theropod

A meat-eating dinosaur that traveled on two legs.

The word "theropod" means "beast-footed."

Triassic

A period of time from about 248 to 205 million years ago.

Dinosaurs first appeared during the Triassic Period.

vertebrate

An animal with a backbone.

All dinosaurs were vertebrates.

volcano

A mountain in which molten lava, ash, and gas erupts through vents.

Some scientists believe a volcano eruption may have caused some dinosaurs to die out.

Pronunciation Key

armor (AR mer)
beak (BEEK)
biped (BY ped)
bone (BOHN)
breed (BREED)
camouflage (KAM uh flahzh)
carnivore (KAR nuh vor)
carnosaur (KAR nuh sor)
club (KLUHB)
cold-blooded
  (KOHLD BLUHD id)
crest (KREST)
Cretaceous (krih TAY shes)
dig site (DIG SITE)
dome head (DOME HED)
egg (EG)
excavate (EK skuh vayt)
extinct (ek STINGKT)
fossil (FOSS uhl)
frill (FRIL)
habitat (HAB uh tat)
herbivore (ER be vor)
horn (HORN)
hunt (HUNT)
Ice Age (ICE AYJ)
Jurassic (jur AS ik)
meteorite (MEET ee eh RYTE)

museum
  (myoo ZEE um)
omnivore (OM nuh vor)
paleontology
  (PAY lee uhn TAHL uh jee)
plates (PLAYTS)
predator (PRED uh ter)
prehistoric (PREE hi STOR ik)
prey (PRAY)
pterosaur (TAYR uh sor)
remains (ri MAYNZ)
reptile (REP tyle)
sauropod (SAWR uh pod)
scales (SKAYLZ)
sense (SENS)
skeleton (SKEL uh tuhn)
skin (SKIN)
skull (SKUHL)
species (SPEE sheez)
tail (TAYL)
talons (TAL uhnz)
teeth (TEETH)
theropod (THAYR uh pod)
Triassic (try AS ik)
vertebrate
  (VER tuh bret)
volcano (vol KAY noh)

29

Did you know...

...dinosaurs were not the largest creatures to have lived? The modern-day blue whale holds that record. Blue whales may grow over 100 feet (30.48 meters) and weigh over 150 tons (136 metric tons).

Did you know...

..."dinosaur" is a Greek word meaning "terrible lizard?"

Did you know...

...dinosaurs were extinct long before humans ever walked the Earth? Dinosaurs died out about 65 million years ago. Prehistoric humans lived about 2 1/2 million years ago.

Did you know...

...dinosaurs first roamed the Earth over 200 million years ago?

Did you know...

...Giganotosaurus is the largest meat-eating dinosaur ever found? Giganotosaurus lived 100 million years ago.

Did you know...

...scientists now believe some dinosaurs may have been warm-blooded? Scientists learn these things by studying rocks and remains from the time of dinosaurs.

Index

Further Reading

Reader's Digest Pathfinders Dinosaurs, Reader's Digest Children's Books Inc., 1999

Whitfield, Philip. *Children's Guide to Dinosaurs and Other Prehistoric Animals,* Simon & Schuster, 1992.

Websites to Visit

www.enchantedlearning.com

www.pbs.org

www.nmnh.si.edu/paleo/dino/

www.nationalgeographic.org

About the Authors

David and Patricia Armentrout specialize in nonfiction writing. They have had several books published for primary school reading. They reside in Cincinnati, Ohio, with their two children.